THE Animal HALL OF FAME
Volume 1 By TJ Rob

The Biggest, Smallest, Fastest, Slowest, Meanest, Deadliest, Tallest and MORE...

The ANIMAL HALL OF FAME — Volume 1
By TJ Rob

Animal Feats and Records Series — Volume 1

Copyright Text TJ Rob, 2016

All rights reserved. No part of the book may be reproduced in any form without permission in writing from the author. Reviewers may quote brief passages in review.

ISBN 978-1-988695-27-3

Disclaimer

No part of this book may be reproduced in any form or by any means, mechanical or electronic, including photocopying or recording, or by an information storage and retrieval system, or transmitted by email without permission in writing from the publisher. This book is for entertainment purposes only. The views expressed are those of author alone.

Published by:
TJ Rob
Suite 609
440-10816 Macleod Trail SE
Calgary, AB T2J 5N8 www.TJRob.com

Image Credit:

pg. 7, By Trebol-a - Own work, CC BY-SA 3.0, https://commons.wikimedia.org/w/index.php?curid=4607913

pg. 23, By Cheryl S. Brehme, USGS - http://soundwaves.usgs.gov/2006/02/pubs.html, Public Domain, https://commons.wikimedia.org/w/index.php?curid=8052018

Pg. 39, By Avispa marina.jpg: Guido Gautsch, Toyota, Japanderivative work: Mithril (talk) - Avispa marina.jpg, CC BY-SA 2.0, https://commons.wikimedia.org/w/index.php?curid=15374006

Photo Credits: Images used under license from Shutterstock.com and Fotolia.com:

Cover page, Svetlana Foote/Shutterstock.com; Cover page, Volodymyr Burdiak/Shutterstock.com; Back Page, Alones/Shutterstock.com; pg. 2, Svetlana Foote/Shutterstock.com; pg. 2, Volodymyr Burdiak/Shutterstock.com; pg. 4, Alones/Shutterstock.com; pg. 5, Alones/Shutterstock.com; pg. 6, Dmitry Pichugin/Fotolia.com; pg. 7, Eric Isselee/Shutterstock.com; pg. 8, Sergey Uryadnikov/Shutterstock.com; pg. 8, Sergey Uryadnikov/Shutterstock.com; pg. 9, Bildagentur Zoonar GmbH/Shutterstock.com; pg. 10, Ryan S Rubino/Shutterstock.com; pg. 11, stockphoto mania/Shutterstock.com; pg. 12, rosesmith/Shutterstock.com; pg. 12, Kletr/Shutterstock.com; pg. 13, Nacho Such/Shutterstock.com; pg. 14, Dmitry Mozhzherin/Shutterstock.com; pg. 15, Tim Ezzy/Shutterstock.com; pg. 16, nattanan726/Shutterstock.com; pg. 17, Sam DCRuz/Shutterstock.com; pg. 18, corlaffra/Shutterstock.com; pg. 19, Computer Earth/Shutterstock.com; pg. 21, Ian Kennedy/Shutterstock.com; pg. 22, meunierd/Shutterstock.com; pg. 23, rickyd/Shutterstock.com; pg. 24, Chris Hill/Shutterstock.com; pg. 25, sivanadar/Shutterstock.com; pg. 26, Christopher Gleockler/Shutterstock.com; pg. 27, Gerckens-Photo-Hamburg/Shutterstock.com; pg. 28, john michael evan potter/Shutterstock.com; pg. 29, Protasov AN/Shutterstock.com; pg. 29, IanRedding/Shutterstock.com; pg. 30, Volt Collection/Shutterstock.com; pg. 31, Karen Sarraga/Shutterstock.com; pg. 32, Catmando/Shutterstock.com; pg. 33, Benjamint/Shutterstock.com; pg. 35, I. Noyan Yilmaz/Shutterstock.com; pg. 35, Dmytro Pylypenko/Shutterstock.com; pg. 35, Andrea Izzotti/Shutterstock.com; pg. 36, Mo Wu/Shutterstock.com; pg. 37, Anton Harder/Shutterstock.com

TABLE OF CONTENTS	Page
The Biggest and the Heaviest	4
The Smallest and the Lightest	7
The Fastest	9
The Fastest Bird	10
The Fastest Fish	11
The Slowest	11
The Meanest	14
The World's Deadliest	18
The Loudest	19
The Tallest	20
The Sleepiest	22
The Longest Hibernator	24
The Worst Eyesight	25
The Best Eyesight	26
Hear the Furthest Distance	28
Hear the Quietest Sounds	29
The Best Sense of Smell on Earth	30
The Oldest Living Creatures	31
The Largest Population on Earth	34
The Biggest Jumper	36
The Most Powerful Bite	37
The Most Poisonous Bite/Sting	38
Please leave a review and Other EXCITING books by TJ Rob	40

The Biggest and the Heaviest

The BLUE WHALE

The biggest and heaviest creature EVER to have lived on planet Earth!

200 tons or 400,000 pounds (181,000 kg) in weight.

100 feet (30 meters) long.

Can swim up to 20 miles per hour (32 km per hour).

ENDANGERED SPECIES - only 10,000 to 25,000 left in our oceans.

Lifespan of between 80 to 90 years.

Tongue as big as an Elephant.

Heart as big as a car.

This giant of our oceans feeds on the smallest marine animals - tiny shrimplike animals called krill.

An adult blue whale can eat 7,900 pounds (3,600kg) of krill every day.

The Biggest and the Heaviest
The AFRICAN ELEPHANT

The biggest and heaviest creature on land is a distant second place to the mighty Blue Whale.

Can weigh as much as 2 Rhinos OR 20 Lions — about 15,000 pounds (7,000 kg).

Can stand as high as 13 feet (4 meters) high.

450,000 to 700,000 Elephants are left in the wild in Africa.

Elephants eat for up to 16 hours a day.

They eat over 300 pounds (135 kg) of food a day.

That's like us eating over 150 plates of food in a single day!

Some have been known to move at 25 miles per hour (40 km per hour) for short distances.

They are great walkers and can easily cover 50 miles (80 km) in a single day.

The Smallest and the Lightest
The ETRUSCAN SHREW

Also known as the Etruscan Pygmy Shrew or the White-toothed Pygmy Shrew.

Has a lifespan of 15 months.

Eats mainly insects.

It is considered to be the smallest mammal by weight. It's average weight is less than .1 ounce (2.7 grams).

Lives in forests and brush areas between Southern Asia and Southern Europe.

The Etruscan Shrew's brain is the largest in ratio to its body weight of all animals — larger than even a human's.

The Smallest and the Lightest
The BEE HUMMINGBIRD
The World's SMALLEST bird.

Also known as the Cuban Bee Hummingbird or the Helena Hummingbird.

Lives mostly in Cuba and parts of the West Indies.

Not much bigger than a Bee — that's where it gets it's name!

Average weight of only 0.056 to 0.071 ounces (1.6 to 2 grams) and a length of 2.0 to 2.4 inches (5 to 6 cm).

Eats flower nectar and tiny insects. In a single day a Bee Hummingbird may visit up to 1,500 flowers to collect nectar.

It can beat its wings over 90 times a second — so fast that it can hover over one spot like a helicopter.

The Fastest   The CHEETAH

The World's fastest land animal.

Can reach speeds of 70 miles per hour (113 km/h).

Cheetahs can accelerate from a standstill to 60 miles per hour (96.5 km/h) in less than 3 seconds.

Unlike other cats Cheetahs do not have good night vision. So they only hunt during the day.

Cheetahs cannot roar like Lions. Instead they make growling and purring noises.

Cheetahs are the only big cats that can turn in mid-air while sprinting.

When running, Cheetahs use their tails like a rudder to steer.

The Fastest Bird
The PERRIGRINE FALCON

Exceeds 200 miles per hour (322 km/h) in a hunting dive.

In level flight, they reach speeds of 70 miles per hour (112 km/h).

The body length of a Peregrine Falcon is 13 to 23 inches (34 to 58 cm), and a wingspan of 29 to 47 inches (74 to 120 cm).

Females are 30% larger than males and 50% heavier than males.

Their eyes are so sharp they can spot prey on the ground from 1000 feet (300 meters) up.

Females weigh 1.5 to 3.5 pounds (.75 to 1.5 kg). Males weigh less at between .75 to 2.5 pounds (.33 to 1.15kg).

Peregrine Falcons have a lifespan of about 15 years in the wild.

The Fastest Fish
The SAILFISH

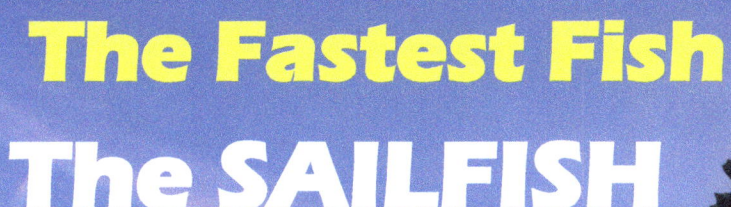

Known for their jumps out of the water.

Can reach speeds of 70 miles per hour (112 km/h).

Sailfish can swim the 100 meter dash in 4.8 seconds, much faster than the best Olympic swimmers.

The sail is kept folded or pushed to one side. When it is threatened, the Sailfish raises its sail to look bigger.

Can weigh up to 200 pounds (90kg) and reach lengths of up to 10 feet (3 meters) long.

Using their nervous system, Sailfish can change their colors almost instantly — from browns, greys, to purple and silver. By changing its color, it can confuse its prey and signal to other Sailfish nearby.

The Slowest
The GARDEN SNAIL

The Garden Snail moves at a top speed of .5 inch (1.3 centimeters) per second. This means that it will take a snail over 20 hours to move .5 mile (800 meters).

A human walking slowly could cover that distance in about 10 minutes.

Although they move incredibly slowly, Garden Snails move at a steady pace.

Garden Snails live up to 5 years, but other species of Snails can live up to 25 years.

The Garden Snail is mainly active during the night or early morning. They are also active on rainy or cloudy days.

When they move, Garden Snails leave a trail of mucus that acts like a lubricant to help "oil" the way for them and reduce friction.

This mucus is not poisonous to humans.

The Slowest
The SLOTH

A Sloth is named after its slowness. Sloth means laziness or sluggishness.

The top speed of a Sloth is about 6.5 feet (2 meters) per minute.

A human could walk that distance in about 1 to 2 seconds.

Sloths live in South and Central America. They are about the size of a small dog or a large cat.

Sloths eat mainly leaves that are not easy to digest. They have a special stomach with different compartments that can take up to a month to fully digest their food.

Sloths only have half the muscle tissue of animals of the same size.

That's why they move so slowly. They are really not lazy.

The Meanest
The SALTWATER CROC

As the world's largest reptile, Saltwater Crocodiles are the most aggressive and dangerous of them all. Even more aggressive than Sharks.

Saltwater Crocodiles see people as food and they will not hesitate to attack and eat them. Sharks might attack people out of curiosity or through mistaken identity.

More than 800 people a year are killed by these creatures.

Saltwater Crocodiles are powerful, fast and smart.

They'll eat anything including Water Buffalo, Monkeys, Wild Boar, and even Sharks.

Average-size males reach 17 feet (5 meters) and 1,000 pounds (450 kilograms) in weight. Crocs of 23 feet (7 meters) long and weighing 2,200 pounds (1,000 kilograms) have been found.

They live in South East Asia and Northern Australia.

The Meanest
The HIPPO

Hippos are the most dangerous animals in Africa, causing more than 3,000 deaths a year. They even kill Crocodiles.

Most large predators won't attack unless agitated, surprised or confused. Hippos will attack without ANY provocation.

A male Hippo will defend its territory which runs along the bank of a river or lake. A female becomes aggressive when defending her young.

A Hippo can weigh as much as 8,000 pounds (3625 kg) with an average weight of about 3,500 pounds (1587 kg).

It can run at speeds of 20 miles per hour (30 km/h) and its mouth can open up to 4 feet high (1.2 meters). Hippos use their mouths to crush like a sledgehammer.

They live in Africa.

The World's Deadliest
The MOSQUITO

Although it is tiny, the Mosquito is the world's deadliest creature. The name Mosquito means "little fly" in Spanish.

Mosquitoes can carry deadly diseases. The worst disease they carry is Malaria. More than 600,000 people die every year from Malaria.

More humans die from diseases carried by Mosquitoes than from Snakes, Hippos, Crocs and all other deadly animals added together.

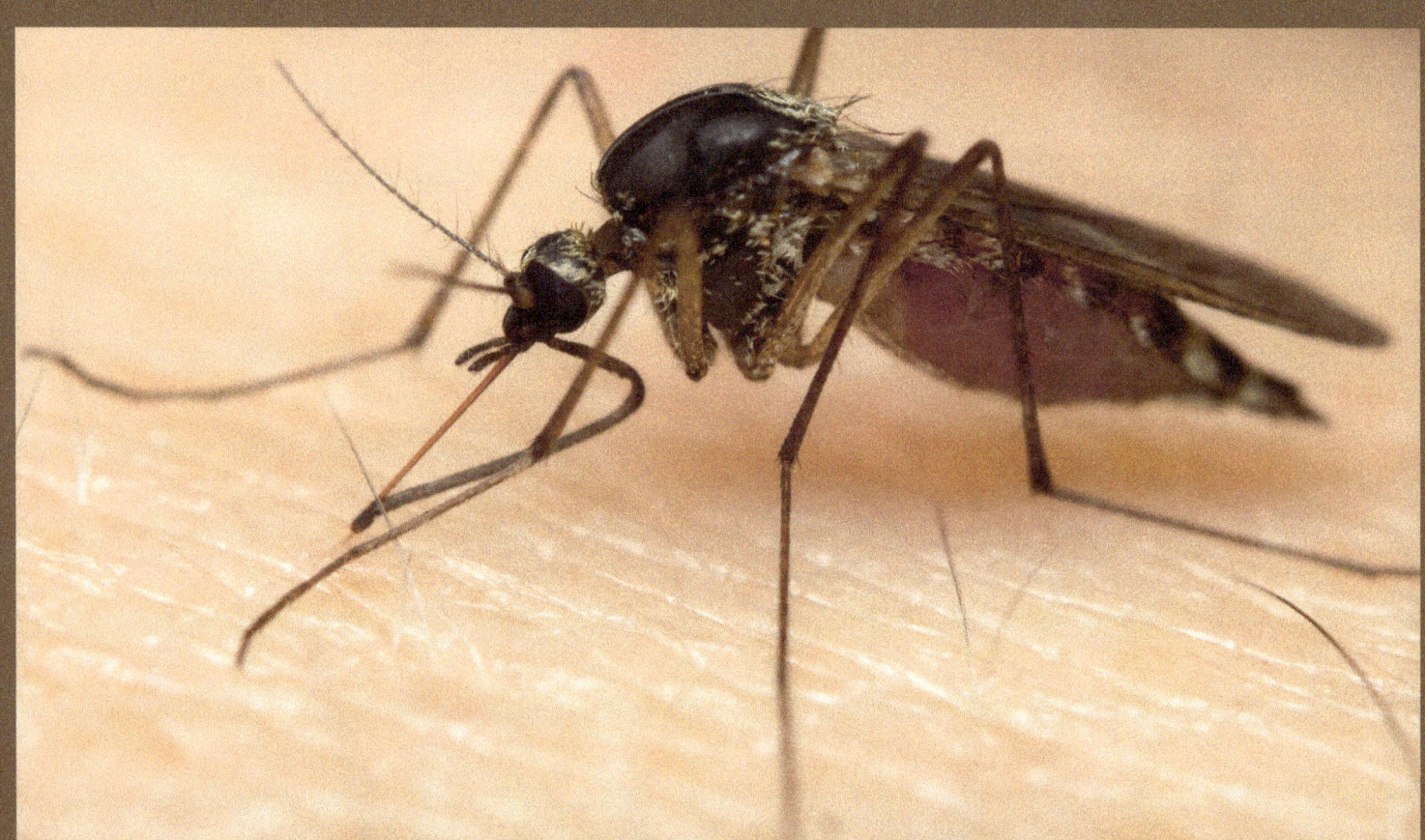

During the breeding season there are so many Mosquitoes that the only creatures that have greater numbers are Ants and Termites. There are over 2,500 different types of Mosquitoes.

Mosquitoes are found in every region on Earth except Antarctica.

The Loudest
The BLUE WHALE

The Biggest and Heaviest creature is also the LOUDEST creature on Earth.

Blue Whales make extremely loud whistling calls called sirens to each other.

These noises can reach up to 188 decibels which is louder than a jet engine or a hand grenade explosion.

Sound underwater travels further than on land. The sounds that Blue Whales make can be heard up to 500 miles (800km) away.

The Tallest

The GIRAFFE

Giraffes are the tallest animals in the world.

Males can grow up to 18 feet (5.5 meters) tall, females can reach 14 feet (4.3 meters) tall. Their babies, called calves, are born six feet (1.8 meters) tall — taller than most humans.

Even with its long neck, a Giraffe has the same number of neck bones as a human. 7 neck bones, but each one is huge. About 10 inches (25 cm) long.

Calves can stand within 20 minutes after birth. After only 10 hours a calf can run alongside its family.

Giraffes spend most of their lives standing up. They sleep and give birth standing up.

With their long legs, Giraffes can run as fast as 35 miles (56 kilometers) an hour over short distances.

They live in Africa and have a lifespan of about 25 years.

The Sleepiest

HAIRY ARMADILLO

The Hairy Armadillo is the champion sleeper in the animal kingdom. It can sleep 20.4 hours every day.

The Sleepiest

LITTLE POCKET MOUSE

Not far behind the Hairy Armadillo is the Little Pocket Mouse. This tiny little mouse sleeps 20.1 hours a day.

KOALA BEAR

Another top sleeper in the animal kingdom is the Koala Bear. It sleeps about 14.5 hours and rests for another 5 hours each day.

The Longest Hibernator
The WOOD FROG

During the cold months of Winter, the Wood Frog hibernates the longest of all creatures — 7 months every year.

Wood Frogs hibernate inside logs or burrows or under rocks or leaf piles.

When they hibernate, they actually stop breathing, their heart stops and ice crystals form in their blood.

When the weather warms, they defrost and their lungs and heart go back to their normal function.

Wood Frogs live in Alaska, Canada and the North Eastern USA.

The WORST EYESIGHT
RHINOS

For their size Rhinos have the worst eyesight.

At a distance of 15 feet (4.5 meters) Rhinos cannot distinguish the difference between objects. Rhinos have such bad vision that they often attack trees and rocks, mistaking them for other animals.

There are other creatures that have poor eyesight, like Moles, Bats and deep sea Fish. Unlike Moles, Bats and deep sea Fish, Rhinos do not live in the dark and are awake during the day.

To make up for their poor eyesight Rhinos do have a good sense of smell and can hear very well too.

The BEST EYESIGHT
EAGLES

Eagles are birds of prey with amazing eyesight.

Eagles are able to spot prey on the ground from 2 miles (3.2km) away. They are even able to spot fish swimming underwater.

Their eyesight is 4 to 8 times better than human vision.

Eagles see colors more brightly than we do.

They are also able to move each eye separately from one another.

An Eagle only weighs 10 pounds (4.5kg), but has the same size eye as a human weighing 200 pounds (91 kg).

HEAR the furthest distance
ELEPHANTS

Elephants can hear sounds at very low frequencies – 20 times lower than our human ear can detect. Elephants can hear each other from 4 miles (6.5 km) away.

Even more amazing, Elephants can detect the rumbling sound of thunder from over 100 miles (160 km) away.

Scientists have recorded Elephants in Namibia hearing a storm from 170 miles (273 km) away. The Elephants changed direction towards the storm to find the water and the new plant growth from the rain.

HEAR the quietest sounds
GREATER WAX MOTH

The Greater Wax Moth has the most super sensitive hearing of all creatures on Earth.

It can hear 150 times better than we do.

The Moth has evolved to hear sounds that the super quiet Bat makes to avoid being eaten by them.

The Greater Wax Moth is a favorite food of Bats.

The Best Sense of Smell on Earth
GRIZZLY BEARS

A Grizzly Bear's sense of smell is 2,100 times better than a human's sense of smell.

The part of the brain that is responsible for smell is 5 times larger in a bear's brain than in the brain of a human.

Grizzlies sense of smell is so sensitive that they can smell a dead animal from a distance of 20 miles (32 km) away.

The Oldest Living Creatures
OCEAN QUAHOG   507 years old

The Ocean Quahog is a type of edible Clam that is found in the North Atlantic ocean.

In 2006, an Ocean Quahog was found off the coast of Iceland that was 507 years old.

Scientists count growth bands on the clam's surface to determine the age of these creatures.

Ocean Quahogs are only 3 inches (7.63 cm) across.

They eat microscopic algae.

The Oldest Living Creatures
BOWHEAD WHALE

The runner up for longest living animal on earth — 200 plus years.

Bowhead Whales have been found with harpoons in their bodies from about the 1890's. This helps determine their age. Also, Scientists have analyzed the amino acids in these Whales, and have proven that they have a maximum life span of 177 to 245 years.

These Whales have a length of between 46 and 65 feet (14 and 20 meters) long.

The Oldest Living Creatures
GOLAPAGOS TORTOISE

The longest living land animal — 180 years.

The Galapagos Tortoise is the longest living land animal and also one of the longest living vertebrates (creatures that have a backbone).

These Tortoises can weigh up to 400 pounds (180 kg), and measure 4 feet (1.2 meters) long.

The Galapagos Tortoise is the largest of all the tortoise family. About 15,000 to 20,000 Galapagos Tortoises live only on the Galapagos Islands about 560 miles (900 km) off the West Coast of Ecuador, South America.

Spanish explorers, who discovered the islands in the 16th century, named them after the Spanish word "galápago", meaning tortoise.

The Largest Population on Earth
KRILL

The champion for the largest population of animals on Earth is Krill, with a population size of 500 trillion animals (500,000,000,000,000).

Krill is a tiny animal in the Crustacean family (Shrimps, Lobster, Crabs, Crayfish). Krill is a Norwegian word meaning "small fry of fish".

Krill is the favorite food of Baleen and Blue Whales. It is also eaten by Seals, Penguins, Squid and Fish.

More than 150,000 tons of Krill is harvested by humans each year. It is used for bait, aquarium food, food for farmed fish and by the drug industry.

Krill are swarming animals. They live in huge swarms of millions of animals together in all the Oceans on the planet.

Krill can live from 6 months up to 6 years, depending on the species.

The Biggest Jumper
The RED KANGAROO

The Red Kangaroo is the world's biggest jumper. It can jump 30 feet (9 meters) in a single hop.

It cannot move its legs separately from one another. So it hops.

It hops fast too — up to 35 miles per hour (56 km/h).

Red Kangaroos grow up to 5 feet (1.5 meters) in length and can weigh up 200 pounds (91 kg).

A baby is called a Joey and a group of kangaroos is called a Mob.

Red Kangaroos live in Australia and can live up to 23 years old in the wild.

The Most Powerful Bite
The SALTWATER CROC

Animal bites are measured in "pounds per square inch" (PSI). This is the force as their jaw closes when they bite. The higher the PSI number the more powerful the bite.

A Dog has a bite force of around 200 to 300 PSI.

The bite champion on Earth is the Saltwater Crocodile of Australia, the largest of all crocodiles. This reptile has a bite force of up to 7,700 PSI.

This would be enough to crush the skull of an adult cow.

Saltwater Crocs have a much greater bite force than a great White Shark, a Lion, a Tiger or even a Hippo.

The Most Poisonous Bite/Sting

The BOX JELLYFISH

The Box Jellyfish is the world's number one most poisonous animal. It is mainly found in the Northern Ocean of Australia and Southern Coast of Queensland, Australia.

It is difficult to spot a Box Jellyfish in the water because it looks transparent.

The toxins of Box Jellyfish attack the nervous system, heart and skin cells. Its sting is so powerful and so painful that a victim dies of shock, drowning or of heart failure. Death often occurs within 2 to 3 minutes after being stung.

The Box Jellyfish have shells measuring 7 inches (17.75 cm) long and have 15 tentacles on each side of their body. The tentacles can reach up to 10 feet (3 meters) long.

Each tentacle contains more than 5000 stinging cells.

Hundreds of fatal attacks on humans by Box Jellyfish are reported every year.

There are very few cases of people surviving its poison.

THANKS FOR READING!

Please leave a review at the website where you bought this book and tell others what you liked about it.

Visit www.TJRob.com for a FREE eBook and to see TJ Rob's other exciting books

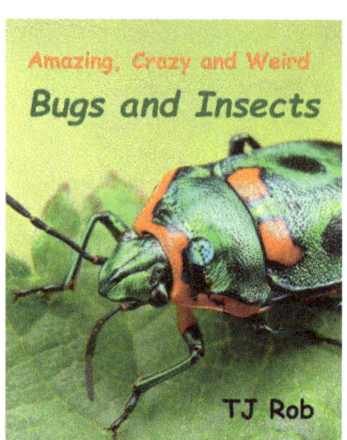

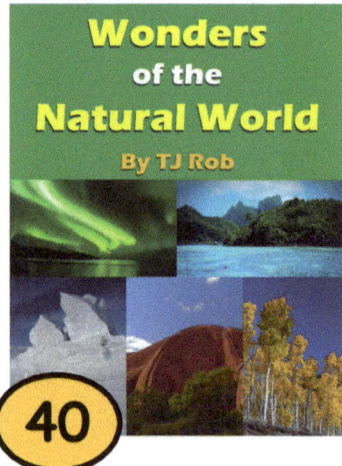
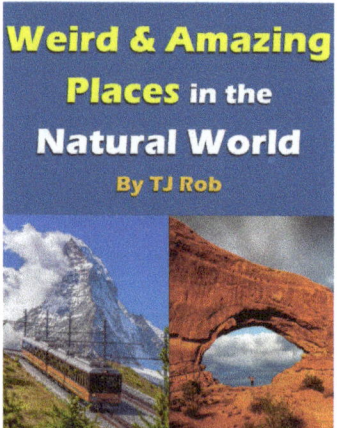

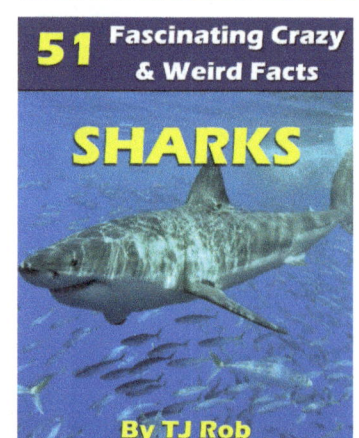

www.ingramcontent.com/pod-product-compliance
Lightning Source LLC
Chambersburg PA
CBHW040005080526
44586CB00027B/2889